ROALD ~

~ OX1 1BY

.oxcoll.com

EDWARD
THE CONQUEROR
and Other Stories

The vocabulary is based on
Michael West: A General Service List of
English Words, revised & enlarged edition, 1953
Pacemaker Core Vocabulary, 1975
Salling/Hvid: English-Danish Basic Dictionary, 1970
J. A. van Ek: The Threshold Level for Modern Language
Learning in Schools, 1976

Series editor: Ulla Malmmose

Cover photo: © Thomas Berthelsen, Billedhuset
Cover layout: Mette Plesner

Editor: Solveig Odland
Illustrations: Oskar Jørgensen

Easy Readers EGMONT

Printed in Denmark by
Sangill Grafisk, Holme-Olstrup

ROALD DAHL

was born on September 13, 1916 in South Wales of Norwegian parents. His father, who was a shipbroker, died four years later.

After he left school in 1932, he spent some months on an expedition exploring in Newfoundland. At eighteen he joined the Shell Oil Company in London. After training, the company sent him to Dar-es-Salaam, Tanganyika.

When the war broke out he drove 1,000 miles to Nairobi to volunteer for the RAF. He joined a fighter squadron in the Lybian desert where he was severely wounded. In 1942 he was sent to Washington as Assistant Air Attaché to the British Embassy.

There he began to write short stories. The first twelve, all about flying, were sold to major American magazines and were later published in a book "Over to You" in 1946.

He got himself removed from the Embassy into the more exciting field of Intelligence. He left the RAF at the end of the war with the rank of Wing Commander.

He married actress Patricia Neal in 1953. They have four children.

Roald Dahl has twice received the Edgar Allan Poe Award ("Edgar") of Mystery Writers in America.

Writings: "The Gremlins" (a juvenile) 1943; "Over to You" (story collection) 1946; "Sometime Never, a Fable for Supermen", 1948; "Someone Like You", 1953; "Kiss, Kiss" (story collection) 1960; "James and the Giant Peach" (children's book) 1964, filmed as "Willy Wonka and the Chocolate Factory"; "Switch Bitch" (story collection) 1974; "Danny and the Champion of the World" (children's book) 1976; "The Wonderful Story of Henry Sugar & Six More", 1977; "The Enormous Crocodile", 1978. He is also the author of the script "You Only Live Twice", a James Bond film. Roald Dahl owes part of his large American following to his CBS-TV series "Way Out".

CONTENTS

Nunc Dimittis 5

Royal Jelly 39

Edward the Conqueror 72

Nunc Dimittis*

It is nearly midnight. I can see that if I don't make a start with writing this story now, I never shall. All evening I have been sitting here trying to force myself to begin. But the more I have thought about it, the more shocked and *ashamed* I have become by the whole thing.

My idea – and I believe it is a good one – is to try, by examining all the events, to discover a reason for the awful thing I did to Janet de Pelagia. All I hope for is a gentle and understanding listener to whom I can address myself and tell every detail of this sad story.

To be quite honest, I must admit that what is disturbing me most is not so much the sense of my own *shame,* or even the hurt I have caused poor Janet. It is the knowledge that I have made a terrible fool of myself and that all my friends – if I can still call them that – all those warm and friendly people who used to come so often to my house, must be regarding me as an evil, *vindictive* old man. Yes, that is what really hurts. When I say to you that my friends are my whole life – everything, absolutely everything in it – then perhaps you will begin to understand.

Or will you? I doubt it – unless I first tell you the sort of person I am.

---

* Beginning of religious song meaning, 'Now I'm ready to die.' (St. Luke, 2.29)

ashamed, feeling *shame* (see below)

shame, a feeling of having done something wrong

vindictive, wanting to hurt in return for harm received

5

Well – let me see. Now that I come to think of it, I suppose I am, after all, a type that is seldom met. The rich, middle-aged man of *culture,* loved by his many friends for his charm, his money, his learning, and I hope for himself also. You find this type of man only in the big capitals – London, Paris, New York, of that I am certain. The money he has was earned by his dead father whose memory he looks down upon. He secretly hates all people who never learned the difference between Rockingham and Spode*, Sheraton and Chippendale**, Monet or Manet***, or even Pommard and Montrachet****.

He possesses above all things an excellent taste. He has the finest collection of paintings by Constable, Lautrec, Cézanne, just to mention a few. Among these walls on which these wonders hang, he lives and moves and gives his parties.

He is, of course, not married, nor does he ever appear to get *entangled* with the women who surround him and who love him so dearly.

I don't think I need say any more. You should know

porcelain

---

culture, here, good taste in art, music, literature etc.
*types of *porcelain* (see picture)
**styles of chairs, tables etc.
***French painters
****Burgundy wines
entangled, mixed up

me well enough by now to judge me fairly – and dare I hope? – to feel sympathy with me when you hear my story. You may even decide that much of the blame for what has happened should be placed, not upon me, but upon a lady called Gladys Ponsonby. After all, she was the one who started it. Had I not seen Gladys Ponsonby back to her house that night nearly six months ago, and had she not spoken so freely to me about certain people, and certain things, then this sad business would never have taken place.

It was last December, if I remember rightly. I had been dining with the Ashendens in that lovely house of theirs that overlooks the southern part of Regent's Park. There were a fair number of people there, but Gladys Ponsonby was the only one beside myself who had come alone. So when it was time for us to leave, I naturally offered to see her safely back to her house. We left together in my car. When we arrived at her place she asked me to come in and have »one for the road«, as she put it. I didn't like the idea but I didn't wish to seem *stuffy*, so I told the *chauffeur* to wait and followed her in.

Gladys Ponsonby is a very short woman, certainly not more than four foot nine or ten, maybe even less than that. When I am beside her she gives me the funny feeling that I am standing on a chair.

She is a *widow*, a few years younger than me – maybe fifty-three or four, and it is possible that thirty years ago she was quite a charming little thing. But

---

stuffy, without feeling or understanding
chauffeur, driver
widow, woman whose husband is dead

now her face is loose, the eyes, the nose, the mouth are buried in folds of fat so that one does not notice them. Except perhaps the mouth, which reminds me – I cannot help it – of a fish.

As she gave me my *brandy* in the living-room, I noticed that her hand wasn't steady. The lady is tired, I told myself, so I musn't stay long. We sat down and for a while discussed the Ashendens' party and the people who were there. Finally I got up.

'Sit down, Lionel,' she said. 'Have another brandy.'

'No, really, I must go.'

---

brandy, spirit made from wine

'Sit down and don't be so stuffy. I'm having another one. The least you can do is keep me company while I drink it.'

I watched her as she crossed the room to get the drink, *swaying* a little and holding her glass out in front of her with both hands. The sight of her walking like that, so short and fat, suddenly gave me the funny idea that she had no legs at all above the knees.

She half turned to look at me as she poured the drink, and some of it went over the side of the glass.

'Tell me what you think of my new *portrait.*' She nodded at a large picture hanging over the fireplace that my eye had been trying to avoid ever since I entered the room. It was a *hideous* thing, painted, as I well knew, by a man who was now very popular in London, a very *mediocre* painter called John Royden. It was a full-length portrait of Gladys, Lady Ponsonby, painted with a certain skill to make her out to be a tall and quite lovely creature.

'Charming,' I said.

'Isn't it, though! I'm so glad you like it. I think John Royden is a *genius*. Don't you think he's a genius, Lionel?'

'Well – that might be going a bit far.'

'You mean it's a little early to say for sure?'

'Exactly.'

'But listen, Lionel – I think this will surprise you.

---

sway, to move in a rocking way
portrait, here, a painting of a person
hideous, terrible to look at
mediocre, not very good; ordinary
genius, a particularly clever person

John Royden is so popular now that he won't consider painting anyone for less than a thousand pounds!'

'Really?'

'Oh, yes, everyone's queueing up, simply q u e u e i n g up to get themselves done.'

'Most interesting.'

'Now take your Mr Cézanne or whatever his name is. I'm sure h e never got that sort of money in h i s life-time.'

'Never.'

'And you say h e was a genius?'

'Sort of – yes.'

'Then so is Royden,' she said, settling herself again on the *sofa*. 'The money proves it.'

She sat silent for a while, drinking her brandy, and I couldn't help noticing that her hand still wasn't quite steady. She knew I was watching her, and without turning her head she glanced at me out of the corners of her eyes. 'A penny for your thoughts?'

Now, if there is one expression in the world I cannot stand, it is this. It gives me pain and I can't breathe.

'Come on, Lionel. A penny for them.'

I shook my head, quite *un*able to answer. She turned away and placed the brandy glass on a small table to her left. The manner in which she did this seemed to suggest – I don't know why – that she felt hurt and was now getting ready for action. I waited, rather uncomfortably in the silence that followed. Because I had no conversation left in me, I made great play about smoking my cigar, blowing the smoke up

---

sofa, see picture, page 8
un-, not

slowly towards the ceiling. There was beginning to be something about this lady I did not much like, a *mischievous* air that made me want to get up quickly and go away. When she looked around again, she was smiling at me *slyly* with those little buried eyes of hers, but the mouth – oh, just like that of a fish – was without any expression.

'Lionel, I think I'll tell you a secret.'

'Really, Gladys, I simply must get home.'

'Don't be frightened, Lionel. I won't *embarrass* you. You look so frightened all of a sudden.'

'I'm not very good at secrets.'

'I've been thinking,' she said, 'you know everything about pictures, this ought to interest you.' She sat quite still except for her fingers which were moving all the time, like small white snakes.

'Don't you want to hear my secret, Lionel?'

'It isn't that, you know. It's just that it's so awfully late . . .'

'This is probably the best-kept secret in London. A woman's secret. I suppose it's known to about – let me see – about thirty or forty women altogether. And not a single man. Except him, of course – John Royden. But first of all, promise – p r o m i s e you won't tell anyone?'

'Dear me!'

'You promise, Lionel?'

'Yes, Gladys, all right, I promise.'

---

mischievous, bad, causing trouble
sly, full of tricks
embarrass, to make (someone) feel uncomfortable

'Good! Now listen.' She reached for the brandy glass and settled back comfortably in the far corner of the sofa. 'I suppose you know John Royden paints only women?'

'I didn't.'

'And they're always full-length portraits, either standing or sitting – like mine there. Now take a good look at it, Lionel. Do you see how beautifully the dress is painted?'

'Well . . .'

'Go over and look carefully, please.'

I got up though I didn't really want to and went over and examined the painting. To my surprise I noticed that the paint on the dress was laid on so heavily that it actually raised out from the rest of the picture. It was a trick, quite effective in its way, but neither difficult to do nor entirely original.

'You see?' she said. 'It's thick, isn't it, where the dress is?'

'Yes.'

'But there's a bit more to it than that, you know. I think the best way is to describe what happened the first time I came to John Royden's *studio*.'

Oh, what a *bore* this woman is, I thought, and how can I get away?

'That was about a year ago, and I remember how

beard

---

studio, the workroom of an artist
bore, a dull person or thing, an uninteresting experience

excited I was to be going in to the studio of the great painter. I dressed myself up in a wonderful new thing I'd just got from Norman Hartnell, and a special little red hat, and off I went. Mr Royden met me at the door, and of course I was charmed by him at once. He had a small pointed *beard* and exciting blue eyes, and he wore a *velvet* jacket. The studio was huge, with red velvet sofas, velvet chairs and velvet *curtains* – he loves velvet. He sat me down, gave me a drink and came straight to the point. He told me about how he painted quite differently from other artists. In his opinion, he said, there was only one way to make a perfect painting of a woman's body. I mustn't be shocked when I heard what it was.

curtain

---

velvet, a type of cloth made from silk or cotton with a thick, soft surface

13

"'I don't think I'll be shocked, Mr Royden,' I told him.

"'I'm sure you won't either,' he said. He had very white teeth and they sort of shone through his beard when he smiled. "You see, it's like this," he went on. "You examine any painting you like of a woman – I don't care who it's by – and you'll see that although the dress may be well painted the whole thing looks flat. The dress seems to be hanging on a piece of wood. And you know why?"

"'No, Mr Royden, I don't.'

"'Because the painters themselves didn't really know what was beneath!'"

Gladys Ponsonby paused to have a little more brandy. 'Don't look so shocked, Lionel,' she said to me. 'There is nothing wrong about this. Keep quiet and let me finish. So then Mr Royden said, "That's why I always paint my subjects first of all in the *nude.*"

"'Good Heavens, Mr Royden!' I exclaimed.

"'And when I've done that,' he went on, "we'll have to wait for the paint to dry. Then you come back and I paint on your *underclothes.* And when that's dry, I paint the dress. You see, it's quite simple.'"

'The man is an absolute *rogue!*' I cried.

'No, Lionel, no! You're quite wrong. If only you could have heard him, so charming about it all, and so honest. Anyone could see he really felt what he was saying.'

'I tell you, Gladys, the man's a rogue.'

---

nude, with no clothes on
underclothes, clothes worn under dress
rogue, a person who has no honour

'Don't be so silly, Lionel. And anyway, let me finish. The first thing I told him was that my husband (who was alive then) would never agree.

'"Your husband need never know," he answered. "Why trouble him. No one knows my secret except the women I've painted."

'And when I still objected, I remember he said, "My dear Lady Ponsonby. There is nothing *immoral* about this. Art is never immoral when practised by professionals. It's the same with medicine. You wouldn't refuse to take your clothes off before your doctor, would you?"

'And so he kept on at me about it. I must say, it all sounded quite right, so after a while I gave in and that was that. So now, Lionel, my sweet, you know the secret.' She got up and went over to fetch herself some more brandy.

'Gladys, is this really true?'

'Of course it's true.'

'You mean to say that's the way he paints all his subjects?'

'Yes. And the joke is the husbands never know anything about it. All they see is a nice fully clothed portrait of their wives. Of course, there's nothing wrong with being painted in the nude; artists do it all the time. But our silly husbands have a way of objecting to that sort of thing.'

'Listen, Gladys. I want you to tell me something. Did you by any chance know about this . . . this peculiar *technique* of Royden's before you went to him?'

---

immoral, wrong in a moral sense
technique, here, way of painting

When I asked the question she was in the act of pouring brandy. She stopped and turned her head to look at me, a little smile moving in the corners of her mouth.

'*Damn you,* Lionel,' she said. 'You're far too clever. You never let me get away with a single thing.'

'So you knew?'

'Of course. Hermione Girdlestone told me.'

'Exactly as I thought!'

'There's still nothing wrong.'

'Nothing,' I said. 'Absolutely nothing.' I could see it all quite clear now. This Royden was indeed a rogue. The man knew only too well that there was a whole set of rich women in the city with nothing to do. They got up at noon and spent the rest of the day playing cards and shopping. All they longed for was something exciting to happen, something out of the ordinary, and the more expensive the better. Why – the news of an *entertainment* like this would spread fast among them.

'You won't tell anyone, Lionel, will you? You promised.'

'No, of course not. But now I must go, Gladys. I really must.'

'Don't be so silly. I'm just beginning to enjoy myself. Stay till I've finished this drink, anyway.'

I sat patiently on the sofa while she went on drinking, the little eyes still watching me out of their corners in that mischievous, sly way. I had a strong feeling that the woman was now thinking up some further unpleasant conversation. In the air – although maybe

---

damn you, go to hell!
entertainment, something amusing; fun

I only imagined it – there was a faint smell of danger.

Then suddenly, so suddenly that I jumped, she said, 'Lionel, what's this I hear about you and Janet de Pelagia?'

'Now, Gladys, please . . .'

'Lionel, you're *blushing*!'

'*Nonsense*.'

'Don't tell me the old *bachelor* has really fallen at last?'

'Gladys, don't be silly.' I began making movements to go, but she put a hand on my knee and stopped me.

Don't you know by now, Lionel, that there a r e no secrets?'

'Janet is a fine girl.'

'You can hardly call her a g i r l.' Gladys Ponsonby paused, staring down into the large brandy glass that she held with both hands. 'But of course, I agree with you, Lionel, she's a wonderful person in every way. Except,' and now she spoke very slowly, 'except that she d o e s say some rather peculiar things sometimes.'

'What sort of things?'

'Just things, you know – things about people. About you.'

'What did she say about me?'

'Nothing at all, Lionel. It wouldn't interest you.'

'What did she say about me?'

'It's not worth repeating, honestly it isn't. It's only that it seemed rather strange at the time.'

'Gladys – what did she say?' While I waited for her

---

blush, to go red in the face
nonsense, foolish words
bachelor, an unmarried man

to answer, I could feel the *sweat* breaking out all over my body.

'Well now, let me see. Of course, she was only joking or I couldn't dream of telling you, but I suppose she d i d say how it was all a little bit of a bore.'

'What was?'

'Sort of going out to dinner with you nearly every night – that kind of thing.'

'She said it was a bore?'

'Yes.' Gladys Ponsonby emptied the brandy glass and sat up straight. 'If you really want to know, she said it was a terrible bore. And then . . .'

'What did she say then?'

'Now look, Lionel – there's no need to get excited. I'm only telling you this for your own good.'

'Then please hurry up and tell it.'

'It's just that I happened to be playing cards with Janet this afternoon. I asked her if she was free to dine with me tomorrow. She said no, she wasn't. Well – actually what she said was "I'm dining with that terrible old bore Lionel Lampson."'

'Janet said that?'

'Yes, Lionel dear.'

'What else?'

'Now, that's enough. I don't think I should tell the rest.'

'Finish it, please!'

'Why, Lionel, don't keep shouting at me like that. Of course I'll tell you if you really want to hear it. As a matter of fact, I wouldn't consider myself a true friend

---

sweat, liquid given out through the skin

if I didn't. Don't you think it's the sign of true friendship when two people like us . . .'

'Gladys! P l e a s e hurry!'

'Good heavens, you must give me time to think. Let me see now – so far as I can remember, what she actually said was this . . .' – and Gladys Ponsonby, sitting upright on the sofa with her feet not quite touching the floor, her eyes looking at the wall, began to copy the deep tone of that voice I knew so well – '"Such a bore my dear, because with Lionel one can a l w a y s tell exactly what will happen right from beginning to end. For dinner we'll go to the Savoy Grill – it's a l w a y s the Savoy Grill – and for two hours I'll have to listen to the *pompous* old . . . I mean I'll have to listen to his dull, boring voice talking about pictures and porcelain – a l w a y s pictures and porcelain. Then in the taxi going home he'll reach out for my hand. He'll lean closer and breathe a smell of cigar smoke and brandy into my face talking about how he wished – oh, how he wished he was just twenty years younger. And I will say, 'Could you open a window, do you mind?' And when we arrive at my house I'll tell him to keep the taxi but he will act as if he hasn't heard and pay it off quickly. Then at the front door, while I fish for my key, he'll stand beside me with a begging look in his eyes. I'll slowly put the key in the lock, and slowly turn it. Then – very quickly, before he has time to move – I'll say good night and jump inside and shut the door behind me..." Why, Lionel! What's the matter, dear? You look absolutely ill.'

---

pompous, self-important

At that point, I must have fainted. I can remember practically nothing of the rest of that terrible night. But I have a disturbing feeling that when I came to my senses I broke down completely and permitted Gladys Ponsonby to comfort me in a variety of different ways. Later, I believe I walked out of the house and was driven home. I wasn't clear in my head until I woke up in my bed the next morning.

I awoke feeling weak and shaken. I lay still with my eyes closed, trying to piece together the events of the night before – Gladys Ponsonby's living-room, Gladys on the sofa drinking brandy, the little fat face, the mouth that was like a fish's mouth, the things she said . . . What was it that she had said? Ah, yes. About me. My God, yes! About Janet and me! These terrible, *unbelievable* remarks! Could Janet really have made them? Could she?

I can remember how fast my hate of Janet de Pelagia now began to grow. It all happened in a few minutes – a sudden, strong wave of hate filled me till I thought I was going to burst. I tried to put it away, but it was on me like a fever, and in no time at all I was hunting around for a way to get *revenge*.

A curious way to act, you may say, for a man such as me; to which I would answer – no not really. To my mind, this was the sort of thing that could drive a man to murder. But killing, I decided, was too good for this woman, and far too rough for my own taste. So I began looking for a more clever way to make her suffer.

---

unbelievable, too bad (or good) to be believed
revenge, harm done in return for harm received

Normally I would never make any plans that weren't honest and I have had no practice in it at all. But I was so angry and full of hate that my mind directed all its attention towards this aim. In no time at all a *plot* was forming in my head – a plot so wonderful and exciting that I began to be quite carried away at the idea of it. By the time I had filled in the details my state of mind had changed. My spirits were high, and I remember how I started jumping up and down on my bed like a child. The next thing I knew I had the *telephone directory* in my hands and was searching for a name. I found it, picked up the phone and dialled the number.

'Hello,' I said. 'Mr Royden? Mr John Royden?'
'Speaking.'

---

plot, here, a plan for doing something evil
telephone directory, a book giving names, addresses and telephone numbers

Well – it wasn't difficult to make the man call around and see me for a moment. I had never met him, but of course he knew my name, not only because of my collection of paintings but also as a person of some importance in society.

I jumped out of bed. I felt happy and full of joy all of a sudden. One moment I had been suffering terribly, thinking seriously about killing myself or her, and I don't know what, the next I was singing in my bath. Every now and then I caught myself *rubbing* my hands in evil joy.

At the appointed time Mr John Royden was shown in to my library and I got up to meet him. He was a small *neat* man. He wore a black velvet jacket, a red tie and black shoes. I shook his small neat hand.

'Good of you to come along so quickly, Mr Royden.'

'Not at all, sir.' The man's lips looked wet and were shining *pink* in among all that hair. After telling him how much I liked his work, I got straight down to business.

'Mr Royden,' I said. 'I want you to do something rather unusual for me. It is something quite personal in its way.'

'Yes, Mr Lampson?' He was sitting on a chair opposite me, his head on one side, like a bird.

'Of course, I know I can trust you never to tell anybody what I say.'

'Absolutely, Mr Lampson.'

---

rub, to move (something) against the surface of something else with a certain amount of pressure
neat, well-ordered, with everything in its right place; clean
pink, a colour between red and white

'All right. Now here's what I would like you to do for me: there is a certain lady in town here whose portrait I would like you to paint. I very much want to possess a fine painting of her. However, I have my own reasons for not wishing her to know that it is I who wants and is paying for the portrait.'

'You mean . . .'

'Exactly, Mr Royden. That is exactly what I mean. As a man of the world I'm sure you will understand.'

He smiled, a *crooked* little smile that only just came through his beard, and nodded his head.

'Is it not possible,' I said, 'that a man might be – how shall I put it? – extremely fond of a lady and at the same time have his own good reasons for not wishing her to know about it yet?'

'More than possible, Mr Lampson.'

'Sometimes a man has to wait patiently for the right moment to show his feelings.'

'How right you are, Mr Lampson.'

'All right, Mr Royden. I think you understand. Now – do you happen by any chance to know a lady called Janet de Pelagia?'

'Janet de Pelagia? Let me see now – yes. At least, what I mean is I've heard of her.'

'Do you think you could get to meet her – perhaps at a party or something like that?'

'Shouldn't be too difficult, Mr Lampson.'

'Good, because what I suggest is this: that you go up to her and tell her she's the sort of *model* you've

---

crooked, not honest
model, here, the person who is painted by an artist

been searching for for years – just the right face, the right figure, the right coloured eyes. You know the sort of thing. Then ask her if she'd mind sitting for you free of charge ... Say you would like to do a picture of her for next year's *Academy*. I feel sure she'd be delighted to help you, and honoured too, if I may say so. Then you will paint her and *exhibit* the picture and deliver it to me after the show is over. No one but you need know that I have bought it.'

The small round eyes of Mr Royden were watching me as if he didn't trust me. He looked like a bird the way he was sitting on the edge of his chair.

'There is really nothing wrong about it at all,' I said. 'Just consider it – if you like – a favour to a ... well ... rather *romantic* old man.'

'I know, Mr Lampson, I know ...'

'I'll be glad to pay you double your usual price,' I said quickly.

Academy, (a public show at) a famous art society
exhibit, to show in public
romantic, here, thinking about love

That did it. 'Well, Mr Lampson. I must say this sort of thing's not really in my line, you know. But all the same, I'd have no heart if I said no.'

'I should like a full-length portrait, Mr Royden, please. And I should like her to be standing. That to my mind, is the way she looks best.'

'I quite understand, Mr Lampson. It'll be a pleasure to paint such a lovely lady.'

I expect it will, I told myself. The way you go about it, my boy, I'm quite sure it will. But I said, 'All right, Mr Royden, then I'll leave it all to you. And don't forget – this is a little secret between ourselves.'

When he had gone I forced myself to sit still and take twenty-five deep breaths. Nothing else would have kept me from jumping up and shouting for joy. I have never in my life felt so excited. My plan was working! The most difficult part was already completed. There would be a wait now, a long wait. The way this man painted, it would take him several months to finish the picture. Well, I would just have to be patient, that's all.

I immediately decided that it would be best if I were to go abroad until the picture was finished. So the very next morning, after sending a message to Janet (with whom you may remember I was due to dine that night) telling her I had been called away, I left for Italy.

There, as always, I had a wonderful time, spoiled only by a nervous excitement caused by the thought of returning to the scene of action.

Four months later, in July, on the day of the opening of the Royal Academy, I arrived back. I found to my relief that everything had gone according to plan. The picture of Janet de Pelagia had been painted and hung in the Exhibition. It was already the subject of much talk. I myself did not go to see it, but Royden told me on the telephone that several persons wished to buy it. But they had all been informed that it was not for sale. When the show was over, Royden delivered the picture to my house and received his money.

chandelier

I immediately had it carried up to my workroom, and with growing excitement I began to examine it closely. The man had painted her standing up in a black evening dress under a huge *chandelier*. Her left hand was resting on the back of a heavy red chair.

My God, I thought, what a hideous thing! The portrait itself wasn't so bad. He had caught the woman's expression – the forward drop of the head, the wide blue eyes, the large mouth with a faint smile in one corner. I bent forward to examine the painting of the dress. Yes – here the paint was thicker, much thicker. At this point, unable to wait another moment, I threw off my coat and prepared to go to work.

I should mention here that I have great experience in cleaning and *restoring* paintings. The cleaning, particularly, is a rather simple operation provided one is patient and has a gentle touch. Those professionals who make such a secret of their trade and charge such shocking prices get no business from me. Where my own pictures are concerned I always do the job myself.

I poured out the *turpentine* and added a few drops of *alcohol.* Gently, so very gently, I began to work on the black paint of the dress with this *mixture* on a little *cotton wool.* I could only hope that Royden had

---

restore, to repair (a painting, a building etc.) so as to bring it back to its original condition

turpentine, a liquid used for mixing paints, cleaning paint brushes etc.

alcohol, a spirit

mixture, a number of things mixed together and used for a given purpose

cotton wool, loose cotton pressed into a mass

allowed each *layer* of paint to dry completely before putting on the next. Otherwise the two would mix, and what I had in mind would be impossible. Soon I would know. I was working on one square inch of black dress somewhere around the lady's stomach and I took plenty of time. I carefully tested the paint, adding a drop or two more of alcohol to my mixture until finally it was strong enough. The paint began to come off.

For perhaps a whole hour I worked away on this little square, rubbing more and more gently, as I came closer to the layer below. Then, a small pink spot appeared, and little by little it spread until the whole of my square inch was a clear shining pink.

Now I knew that the black paint could come off without disturbing what was beneath. So long as I was patient and hard-working I would easily be able to take it all off. Also, I had discovered the right mixture to use and just how hard I could safely rub, so things would go much quicker now.

I must say it was rather an amusing business. I worked first from the middle of her body down, and as the lower half of her dress came away bit by bit a strange piece of *underwear* began to show. I didn't for the life of me know what the thing was called. It was an unbelievable *apparatus* made of what appeared to be a strong *elastic* material. Its purpose seemed to be to contain the woman's filled out body and force it into a

---

layer, covering
underwear, underclothes
apparatus, object made for a special purpose
elastic, able to stretch

28

neat shape. As I travelled lower and lower down, I came upon a striking arrangement of *straps,* also pink. They were fastened to this elastic thing and hung four or five inches down to hold the tops of the stockings.

Quite fantastic the whole thing seemed to me as I stepped back to examine it. Did all women use such tricks? I felt rather bad about it. Had I not, during all these past months, believed this lady to have a lovely figure?

When the whole of the lower half of the dress had come away, I immediately turned my attention to the upper part, working my way slowly up from the lady's middle. First came an area of *naked* body, then higher up the *bosom* itself. And actually containing it, I came upon a piece of apparatus made of heavy black material edged with *lace*. This, I knew very well, was the *brassiere* – another frightening instrument upheld

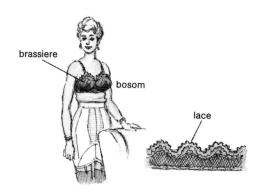

---

strap, a narrow band used to fasten objects and hold them in place
naked, with no clothes on

by an arrangement of black straps, as scientifically arranged as *cables* on a *suspension bridge*.

Dear me, I thought, one lives and learns.

But now at last the job was finished, and I stepped back again to take a final look at the picture. It was truly a surprising sight: this woman, Janet de Pelagia, almost life size, standing there in her underwear – in a sort of drawing-room, I suppose it was – with a great chandelier above her head and a red chair by her side. She herself – this was the most disturbing part of it all – looked so completely unconcerned, with the wide blue eyes, the faint smile of the large mouth. Also I noticed, something of a shock, that she was extremely bow-legged, like people who often ride on horseback. I tell you openly, the whole thing embarrassed me. I felt as though I had no right to be in the room, certainly no right to stare. So after a while I went out and shut the door behind me. It seemed like the only proper thing to do.

Now, for the next and final step! And do not imagine simply because I have not mentioned it for a while that my desire for revenge had grown less during the last few months. Just the opposite, it had if anything increased. With the last act about to be performed, I can tell you I found it hard to contain myself. That night, for example, I didn't go to bed.

You see, I couldn't wait to get the *invitations* out. I sat up all night preparing them. There were twenty-two of them in all, and I wanted each to be a personal

---

cable, a metal line
suspension bridge, a bridge held up by cables
invitation, a note or message used for inviting people

note. "I'm having a little dinner on Friday night, the twenty-second, at eight. I do hope you can come along . . . I'm so looking forward to seeing you again . . ."

The first, the most carefully written, was to Janet de Pelagia. I told her I was sorry not to have seen her for so long . . . I had been abroad . . . It was time we got together again, etc., etc. The next was to Gladys Ponsonby. Then one to Hermione Lady Girdlestone, another to Princess Bicheno, Mrs Cudbird, Sir Hubert Kaul, Mrs Galbally, Peter Euan-Thomas, James Pisker, Sir Eustace Piegrome, Peter van Santen, Elizabeth Moynihan, Lord Mulherrin, Bertram Sturt, Philip Cornelius, Jack Hill, Lady Akemann, Mrs Icely, Humphrey King-Howard, Johnny O'Coffey, Mrs Uvary, and the Dowager Countess of Waxworth.

All the guests were carefully chosen. They were the most distinguished men and women in the top of our society.

I knew very well that a dinner at my house was regarded as quite an occasion; everybody liked to come. And now, as I watched the point of my pen moving quickly over the paper, I could almost see the ladies in their pleasure picking up their bedside telephones the morning the invitations arrived . . . "Lionel's giving a party . . . he's asked you too? My dear, how nice . . . his food is always so good . . . and s u c h a lovely man, isn't he though, yes . . ."

Is that really what they would say? It suddenly came to my mind that it might not be like that at all. More like this perhaps: "I agree, my dear, yes, not a bad old man . . . but a bit of a bore, don't you think? . . . What did you say? . . . dull? But terribly, my dear. You've hit the nail right on the head . . . did you ever hear what Janet de Pelagia once said about him? . . . Ah yes, I thought you'd heard that one . . . terribly funny, don't you think . . . poor Janet . . . how she stood it as long as she did I don't know . . ."

Anyway, I got the invitations off, and within a couple of days everybody, with the exception of Mrs Cudbird and Sir Hubert Kaul, who were away, had answered that they would like to come.

At eight-thirty on the evening of the twenty-second, my large drawing-room was filled with people. They stood about the room, drinking their Martinis, talking with loud voices. Janet de Pelagia was wearing the same black dress she had used for the portrait. Every time I caught sight of her, a kind of huge *bubble-*

vision would float up above my head, and in it I would see Janet, bow-legged in her underwear, the black brassiere, the pink elastic belt and straps.

Then we all moved out and entered the dining-room.

'Oh dear, how dark it is in here!' they cried.

'I can hardly see a thing!'

'What lovely little *candles!*'

'But Lionel, how charming!'

There were six thin candles set about two feet apart from each other down the centre of the long table. Their small flames made a little light around the table itself, but left the rest of the room in darkness. It was an amusing arrangement and apart from the fact that it suited my purpose well, it made a pleasant change. The guests soon settled themselves in their right places and the meal began.

They all seemed to enjoy the candlelight and things went very well, though for some reason the darkness caused them to speak much louder than usual. Janet de Pelagia's voice struck me as being particularly loud. She was sitting next to Lord Mulherrin, and I could hear her telling him about the boring time she had had at Cap Ferrat the week before. 'Nothing but Frenchmen,' she kept saying. 'Nothing but Frenchmen in the whole place . . .'

candle

---

bubble-vision, a picture you see in your mind

For my part I was watching the candles. They were so thin that I knew it would not be long before they burned down to their bases. Also I was terribly nervous – I will admit that – but at the same time very excited. Every time I heard Janet's voice or caught sight of her face in the light of the candles, there was a sudden feeling of *excitement* which ran under my skin like fire.

At last the time had come. I took a deep breath and in a loud voice I said, 'I'm afraid we'll have to have the lights on now. The candles are nearly finished. Mary,' I called. 'Oh Mary, switch on the lights, will you please.'

There was a moment of silence. I heard the maid walking over to the door, then the short sound of the switch and the room was flooded with light. They all closed their eyes, opened them again, looked about them.

At this point I got up from my chair and slipped quietly from the room. As I went I saw a sight that I shall never forget as long as I live. It was Janet, with both hands in the air, stopped, frozen still, caught in the act of *gesticulating* towards someone across the table. Her mouth had dropped open two inches. She wore the surprised, not-quite-understanding look of a person who exactly one second before has been shot dead, right through the heart.

In the hall outside I paused and listened to the noise, the cries of the ladies and the angry, unbelieving shouts of the men. Soon everybody was talking or

---

excitement, the state of being excited
gesticulate, to express oneself with arms and hands

34

shouting at the same time. Then – and this was the sweetest moment of all – I heard Lord Mulherrin's voice, roaring above the rest, 'Here! Someone! Hurry! Give her some water quick!'

Out in the street the chauffeur helped me into my car. Soon we were away from London and running happily towards this, my other house, which is only ninety-five miles from town anyway.

The next two days I spent *gloating*. I walked around in a dream of pleasure, extremely satisfied with myself. It wasn't until this morning when Gladys Ponsonby called me on the phone that I suddenly came to my senses. I realised that I was not a hero at all but an *outcast*. She informed me – with what I thought was just a faint note of delight – that every-body, all my old loving friends were saying the most terrible things about me. Also they had declared that they would never never speak to me again. Except her, she kept saying. Everybody except her. And didn't I think it would be rather nice, she asked, if she could come down and stay with me a few days to cheer me up?

I'm afraid I was too *upset* by that time to answer her. I put the phone down and went away to *weep*.

Then at noon today came the final blow. The post arrived, and with it – I can hardly bring myself to write about it, I am so ashamed – came a letter, the sweetest little note from none other than Janet de

---

gloat, to look at or think about with evil joy
outcast, a person who is not wanted by his friends or by society
upset, disturbed, troubled
weep, to cry tears

Pelagia herself. She forgave me completely, she wrote, for everything I had done. She knew it was only a joke and I must not listen to the terrible things other people were saying about me. She loved me as she always had and always would to her dying day.

Oh, how terrible I felt when I read this! The more so when I found she had actually sent me by the same post a small present as an added sign of her love – a half-pound glass of my favourite food of all, fresh *caviar*. So although I naturally couldn't eat anything at all at dinner-time this evening, I must admit I ate some of the stuff in an effort to cheer myself up. It is even possible that I took a little too much, because I haven't been feeling any too well this last hour or so. Maybe I should lie down for a while. I can easily come back and finish this later, when I'm in a better shape.

You know – now I come to think of it, I really do feel rather ill all of a sudden . . .

---

caviar, the eggs of a family of large fishes of the northern seas

Questions

1. What sort of a person is Mr Lampson?

2. Why does Gladys Ponsonby invite Lionel Lampson for a drink on that particular night?

3. How is the description of her?

4. What is Mr Lampson's opinion of Mr Royden as a painter?

5. What is the secret of Mr Royden's technique?

6. How does Gladys Ponsonby tell Lionel Lampson about Janet de Pelagia?

7. What may be her reasons for doing this?

8. How does Lionel Lampson plan to get revenge?

9. What happens at his little dinner-party?

10. How do his friends find his joke?

11. What does Gladys Ponsonby feel about this?

12. What is the reason for Lionel Lampson writing his 'letter'?

13. What does Janet de Pelagia have in mind for him?

Royal Jelly*

'It worries me to death, Albert, it really does.' Mrs Taylor said.

She kept her eyes fixed on the baby who was now lying absolutely still in her arms.

'I just know there is something wrong.'

'Try again,' Albert Taylor said.

'It won't do any good.'

'You have to keep trying, Mabel,' he said.

She reached out for the bottle. 'Come on,' she whispered. 'Come on my baby. Wake up and take a bit more of this. Just a little bit, please.'

The husband watched her over the top of his magazine. She looked terribly tired and worried. But even so, as she looked down at the child she was beautiful.

'You see,' she said. 'It's no good. She won't have it.'

She held the bottle up to the light.

royal jelly, a substance produced by *bees,* see picture, page 42

'One *ounce* again. That's all she has taken. No – it isn't even that. It's not enough to keep body and soul together. Albert, it really worries me to death.'

'I know,' he said.

'If only they could find out what was wrong.'

'There's nothing wrong, Mabel! It's just a matter of time.'

'Of course there's something wrong.'

'Dr Robinson says no.'

'Look,' she said, standing up. 'You can't tell me it's natural for a six-week-old child to weigh less, less by more than two whole pounds than she did when she was born! Just look at those legs! They are nothing but skin and bone!'

The *tiny* baby lay in her arms, not moving.

'Dr Robinson said you were to stop worrying, Mabel. So did that other one.'

'Ha!' she said. 'Isn't it wonderful! I'm to stop worrying! What does he want me to do? Treat it as some sort of a joke? I hate doctors! I hate them all!' she cried, and she swung away from him and walked quickly out of the room towards the stairs, carrying the baby with her.

Albert Taylor stayed where he was and let her go.

In a little while he heard her moving about in the bedroom directly over his head with quick nervous footsteps. Soon they would stop, and then he would have to get up and follow her. And when he went into the bedroom he would find her sitting beside the

---

ounce, 1/16 of a pound
tiny, very small

cot as usual, staring at the child and crying softly.

'She's *starving,* Albert,' she would say.

'Of course she's not starving.'

'She i s starving. I know she is and I believe you know it too, but you won't admit it. Isn't that right?'

Every night now it was like this.

Last week they had taken the child back to the hospital, and the doctor had examined her carefully and told them that there was nothing the matter.

'It took me nine years to get this baby, Doctor,' Mabel had said. 'I think it would kill me if anything should happen to her.'

That was six days ago and since then she had lost another five ounces.

But worrying about it wasn't going to help anybody, Albert Taylor told himself. One simply had to trust the doctor on a thing like this. He picked up his magazine and looked down the list of contents to see what it had to offer this week:

Among the Bees in May

The Latest in Royal Jelly

British Beekeepers *Annual* Dinner

Association News

All his life Albert Taylor had been fascinated by anything that had to do with bees. As a small boy he used often to catch them in his hands and go running with them into the house to show his mother. Sometimes he would put them on his face and let

---

cot, a small bed with high sides for a child
starve, to die, or suffer greatly, from hunger
annual, happening every year

them run all over it. He never got *stung,* the bees seemed to enjoy being with him.

By the time he was twelve he had built his first *hive.* Two years later he had no less than five hives standing neatly in a row against the fence in his father's small back yard.

He never had to use smoke when there was work to do inside a hive, and he never wore *gloves* on his hands or a net over his head. Clearly there was some strange

mandibles   bee   sting   gloves

sting, to wound by means of a *sting*
hive, a box etc. where bees live and store up *honey* (see p. 43)

sympathy between this boy and the bees. Down in the village, in the shops and pubs, they began to speak about him with a certain kind of respect, and people started coming up to the house to buy his *honey*.

When he was eighteen he rented one *acre* of ground down the valley about a mile from the village, and there he had set out to start his own business. Now, eleven years later, he was still on the same spot, but he had six acres of ground instead of one, two hundred and forty hives, and a small house that he'd built with his own hands. He had married at the age of twenty and that, apart from the fact that it had taken them over nine years to get a child, had also been a success. In fact, everything had gone pretty well for Albert until this strange little baby girl came along and started frightening them by refusing to eat properly and losing weight every day.

He looked up from his magazine and began thinking about his daughter.

That evening, when she had opened her eyes at the beginning of the feed, he had looked into them and seen something that frightened him to death – a *vacant* stare, as though the eyes themselves were not connected to the brain at all.

Did those doctors really know what they were talking about? One could always take her to another hospital, somewhere in Oxford perhaps. He might suggest that to Mabel when he went upstairs.

He switched his attention back to the magazine and

---

honey, a sweet substance produced by the bees
acre, measure of land
vacant, empty; showing no thoughts or interest

went on with his reading. The article was called, 'The Latest on Royal Jelly'. He doubted very much whether there would be anything in this that he didn't know already:

"What is the wonderful substance called royal jelly?"

He reached for his pipe on the table beside him and began filling it, still reading.

"Royal jelly is produced by nurse bees to feed the *larvae* immediately they have *hatched* from the egg ..."

All old stuff, he told himself, but for want of anything better to do, he continued to read.

"Royal jelly is fed to all bee larvae for the first three days after hatching from the egg. But beyond that point only the larvae which are going to become queens are fed throughout the whole of their *larval* period on pure royal jelly. For this reason the name."

Above him, up in the bedroom, the noise of the footsteps had stopped. The house was quiet. He struck a match and put it to his pipe.

"Royal jelly must be a substance of *tremendous nourishing* power for on this substance alone the honey-bee larva increases in weight fifteen hundred times in five days. This is as if a seven-and-a-half pound baby increased in that time to five tons."

Albert Taylor stopped and read that sentence again.

---

larva, pl. *larvae,* an insect at an early state, not yet fully developed
hatch, to break out from the egg
larval, here, as a larva
tremendous, very great in size, amount, power or effect
nourishing, giving the body what is necessary for growth and health

44

"This is as if a seven-and-a-half pound baby . . ."

'Mabel!' he cried, jumping up from his chair. 'Mabel! Come here!'

There was no answer.

He ran up the stairs. The bedroom door was closed. He opened it and stood in the doorway looking into the dark room. 'Mabel,' he said. 'Come downstairs a moment, will you please? I've just had a bit of an idea. It's about the baby.'

She was lying in the dark on her stomach with her arms up over her head. She was crying again.

'Mabel,' he said, going over to her, touching her shoulder. 'Please come down a moment. This may be important.'

'Go away,' she said. 'Leave me alone.'

'Don't you want to hear about my idea?'

'Oh, Albert, I'm t i r e d. I'm so tired I don't know what I'm doing any more. I don't think I can go on. I don't think I can stand it.'

There was a pause. Albert Taylor turned away from her and walked slowly over to the cot where the baby was lying. It was too dark for him to see the child's face, but when he bent down close he could hear the sound of breathing, very faint and quick. 'What is the time for the next feed?' he asked.

'Two o'clock, I suppose.'

'And the one after that?'

'Six in the morning.'

'I'll do them both,' he said. 'You go to sleep and forget all about us. Right?' Already he was carrying the cot out through the door.

'Oh, Albert,' she said.

'Don't you worry about a thing. Leave it to me.'

'Albert . . . I love you.'

'I love you too, Mabel. Now go to sleep.'

Albert Taylor didn't see his wife again until nearly eleven o'clock the next morning when she came rushing down the stairs.

'Albert! Just look at the time! I must have slept twelve hours at least! Is everything all right? What happened?'

He was sitting quietly in his armchair, smoking a pipe and reading the morning paper. The baby was in the cot, sleeping.

'Hullo, dear,' he said smiling.

She ran over to the cot and looked in. 'Did she take anything, Albert? How many times have you fed her? She was due for another one at ten o'clock, did you know that?'

Albert Taylor folded the newspaper neatly and put it away on the side table. 'I fed her at two in the morning,' he said, 'and she took about half an ounce, no more. I fed her again at six and she did better that time, two ounces . . .'

'T w o   o u n c e s! Oh, Albert, that's *marvellous*!'

'And we just finished the last feed ten minutes ago. There's the bottle. Only one ounce left. She drank three. How's that?' He was grinning proudly. 'Doesn't she look better? Doesn't she look fatter in the face?'

'It may sound silly,' the wife said, 'but I actually think she does. Oh, Albert, you're marvellous! How did you do it?'

'She's turning the corner,' he said. 'Just like the doctor said. From now on, you watch her go.'

---

marvellous, wonderful

'I pray to God you're right, Albert.'

'Of course I am. You look a lot better yourself too.'

'I feel wonderful. I'm sorry about last night.'

'Let's keep it this way,' he said. 'I'll do the night feeds in the future. You do all the day ones.'

'No,' she said. 'I wouldn't allow you to do that.'

'Much better we share it.'

'No, Albert. This is my job and I intend to do it. Last night won't happen again.'

There was a pause. 'All right,' Albert said. 'Then I'll do the mixing of the food and getting everything ready. That'll help you a bit, anyway.'

She looked at him carefully, wondering what could have come over him all of a sudden.

'You see, Mabel. I've been thinking that up until last night I've never even raised a finger to help you with this baby.'

'It's very sweet of you, dear, but I really don't think it's necessary . . .'

'Come on!' he cried. 'Don't change the luck! I've done it the last three times and just look what happened. When's the next one? Two o'clock, isn't it?'

'Yes.'

'It's all mixed,' he said. 'Everything is all mixed and ready and all you've got to do when the time comes is to go out to the kitchen and warm it up. That's some help, isn't it?'

The woman got over to him and gave him a kiss. 'You're such a nice man,' she said. 'I love you more and more every day I know you.'

Later in the middle of the afternoon, when Albert was outside in the sunshine working among the hives, he heard her calling to him from the house.

'Albert!' she shouted. 'Albert, come here!' She was running through the grass towards him.

'Oh, Albert! Guess what! I've just finished giving her the two o'clock feed and she's taken the whole lot!'

'No!'

'Every drop of it! Oh, Albert, I'm so happy! She's going to be all right! She's turned the corner just like you said.' She came up to him and threw her arms around his neck and *hugged* him.

'Will you come in and watch the next one and see if she does it again, Albert?'

He told her he wouldn't miss it for anything. She hugged him again, then turned and ran back to the house, singing all the way.

By five-thirty both parents were already seated in the living-room waiting for the six-o'clock feed.

At twenty minutes to six the baby woke up and started screaming its head off.

'There you are!' Mrs Taylor cried. 'She's asking for the bottle. Pick her up quick, Albert, and hand her to me here. Give me the bottle first.'

He gave her the bottle, then placed the baby on the woman's *lap*. The baby immediately began to *suck* with a rapid powerful action, and in seven or eight minutes the entire contents of the bottle disappeared.

'You clever girl,' Mrs Taylor said. 'Four ounces again.'

Albert Taylor looked down at the child.

'Doesn't she seem bigger and fatter to you, Mabel, than she was yesterday?'

'Maybe she does, Albert. I'm not sure. Although actually there couldn't be any real gain in such a short time. The important thing is that she's eating normally.'

'She's turned the corner,' Albert said. 'I don't think you need worry about her any more.'

---

hug, to hold (someone or something) close to oneself with the arms to show love
lap, see picture, page 50
suck, here, to draw milk into the mouth

'I certainly won't.'

They carried the cot and the baby upstairs into the bedroom.

'Doesn't she look lovely, Albert?' whispered the mother. 'Isn't she the most beautiful baby you've ever seen in your entire life?'

'Come on downstairs and cook us a bit of supper,' said Albert.

After they had finished eating, the parents settled themselves in armchairs in the living-room, Albert with his magazine and his pipe, Mrs Taylor with her *knitting*. But the scene was very different from the night before. Mrs Taylor was smiling with pleasure and her eyes were shining. Every now and again she

lap

knitting

would look up from her knitting and smile lovingly at her husband.

'Albert,' she said after a while.

'Yes, dear?'

'What was it you were going to tell me last night when you came rushing up to the bedroom? You said you had an idea for the baby.'

Albert Taylor put the magazine down on his lap and gave her a long *sly* look.

'Did I?' he asked.

'Yes.' She waited for him to go on, but he didn't.

'What's the big joke?' she asked. 'Why are you grinning like that?'

'It's a joke all right,' he said.

'Tell it to me, dear.'

'I'm not sure I ought to,' he said. 'You might say that I'm lying.'

She had seldom seen him looking so pleased with himself as he was now, and she smiled back at him, inviting him to continue.

'I'd just like to see your face when you hear it, Mabel, that's all.'

'Albert, what i s all this?'

'You do think the baby's better, don't you?' he asked.

'Of course I do.'

'That's good,' he said with a wide grin. 'You see, it's me that did it.'

'Did what?'

'I *cured* the baby.'

---

sly, here, giving the idea that he is wiser than she thinks
cure, to free from disease

'Yes, dear, I'm sure you did.' Mrs Taylor went on with her knitting.

'Then how did I do it?'

'Well,' she said, pausing a moment to think. 'I suppose it's simply that you're very good at mixing the feeds. Ever since you started she's got better and better.'

'You mean there's some sort of art in mixing the feeds?'

'I suppose there is.' She was knitting away and smiling to herself, thinking how funny men were.

'I'll tell you a secret,' he said. 'You're absolutely right. Although, mind you, it isn't so much h o w you mix it that counts. It's what you put in it. You realise that, don't you, Mabel?'

Mrs Taylor stopped knitting and looked sharply at her husband. 'Albert,' she said, 'don't tell me you've been putting things into that child's milk?'

He sat there grinning.

'Well, have you or haven't you?'

'It's possible,' he said.

'Albert,' she said. 'Stop playing with me like this. You haven't r e a l l y put anything into her milk, have you? Answer me properly, Albert. This could be serious with such a tiny baby.'

'The answer is yes, Mabel.'

'A l b e r t T a y l o r! How could you?'

'Now don't get excited,' he said. 'I'll tell you all about it if you really want me to.'

'It was beer!' she cried. 'I just know it was beer!'

'Don't be so silly, Mabel, please.'

'Then what was it?'

Albert laid his pipe down carefully on the table

beside him and leaned back in his chair. 'Tell me,' he said, 'did you ever by any chance happen to hear me mentioning something called royal jelly?'

'I did not.'

'It's *magic*,' he said. 'Pure magic. Last night I suddenly got the idea that if I was to put some of it into the baby's milk . . .'

'How d a r e you!'

'Now, Mabel, you don't even know what it is yet.'

'I don't care what it is,' she said. 'You can't put foreign bodies like that into a tiny baby's milk. You must be mad.'

'It does no harm, Mabel, otherwise I wouldn't have done it. It comes from bees.'

'I might have guessed that.'

'And it's so *precious* that practically no one can afford to take it. When they do, it's only a little drop at a time.'

'And how much did you give our baby, might I ask?'

'Ah,' he said, 'that's the whole point. That's where the difference lies. I believe that our baby, just in the last four feeds, has already had about fifty times as much royal jelly as anyone else in the world has ever taken before. How about that?'

'Albert, you're joking.'

'I swear it,' he said proudly.

She sat there staring at him, her mouth slightly open.

---

magic, any influence that produces results that cannot be explained

precious, of great price or value

'You know what this stuff actually costs, Mabel, if you want to buy it? There's a place in America where they sell it at this very moment for something like five hundred dollars a pound! Five hundred dollars! That's more than gold, you know.'

She hadn't the faintest idea what he was talking about.

'I'll prove it,' he said. He jumped up and went across to the large bookcase where he kept all his literature about bees. He took down a number of "The American Bee *Journal*" and turned to a page at the back.

journal, magazine

'Here you are,' he said. 'Exactly as I told you. This is an actual shop in New York, read it: "We sell royal jelly – $ 480 per pound."'

'It doesn't say you can go putting it into the milk of a practically new-born baby,' she said. 'I don't know what's come over you, Albert, I really don't.'

'It's curing her, isn't it?'

'I'm not sure about that, now.'

'Don't be so damn silly, Mabel. You know it is.'

'Then why haven't other people done it with their babies?'

'I keep telling you,' he said. 'It's too expensive. Practically nobody in the world can afford to buy royal jelly just for eating. The people who buy it are the big companies that make women's face creams and things like that. They mix a tiny bit of it into the face cream and it sells like hot cakes for very high prices. Anyway, that's not the point. The point is this. It's done so much good to our little baby just in the last few hours that I think we ought to go right on giving it to her. I've got two hundred and forty hives out there and if I turn over maybe a hundred of them to making royal jelly, we ought to be able to supply her with all she wants.'

'Albert Taylor,' the woman said, stretching her eyes wide and staring at him. 'Have you gone out of your mind? I forbid it. You're not to give my baby another drop of that awful jelly, you understand?'

'Now, Mabel . . .'

'And quite apart from that, we had a shocking honey crop last year. If you go fooling around with those hives now, there's no telling what might not happen.'

'There's nothing wrong with my hives, Mabel.'

'You know very well we had only half the normal crop last year.'

'Do me a favour, will you?' he said. 'Let me explain some of the marvellous things this stuff does.'

'You haven't even told me what it is yet.'

She sighed and picked up her knitting once more.

'You know, don't you,' he said, 'that each colony has only one queen?'

'Yes.'

'And the queen lays all the eggs?'

'Yes, dear. That much I know.'

'All right. Now the queen can actually lay too different kinds of eggs. You didn't know that, but she can. She can lay eggs that produce *drones,* and she can lay eggs that produce workers. The drones are the *males.* We don't have to worry about them. The workers are all *females.* The workers cannot lay eggs, but the queen can. She can actually lay her own weight in eggs in a single day. Now what happens is this. The queen lays her eggs in what we call *cells.* You know all those hundreds of little holes you see in a

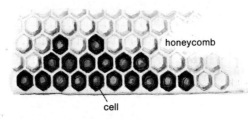

honeycomb

cell

---

drone, a *male* bee (see below)
male/female, (he/she) the two classes into which human beings and animals are divided according to the part they play in producing children or young

56

honeycomb? Well, a *brood comb* is just about the same except the cells don't have honey in them, they have eggs. She lays one egg in each cell, and in three days each of these eggs hatches out into a tiny *grub* called a larva.

Now, as soon as this larva appears, the nurse bees – they're the young workers – all crowd round and start feeding them like mad. And you know what they feed it on?'

'Royal jelly,' Mabel answered patiently.

'Right!' he cried. 'That's exactly what they do feed it on. They make this substance themselves and start putting it into the cell to feed the larva. And what happens then?'

He paused, looking at her with his small grey eyes. Then he turned slowly in his chair and reached for the magazine that he had been reading the night before.

'You want to know what happens then?' he asked, wetting his lips.

'I can hardly wait.'

'"Royal jelly,"' he read, '"must be a substance of tremendous nourishing power, for on this substance alone, the honeybee larva increases in weight f i f t e e n h u n d r e d t i m e s in five days!"'

'How much?'

'Fifteen hundred times, Mabel. And you know what that means if you put it in terms of a human being? It means,' he said in a low voice, leaning forward, fixing her with those small pale eyes, 'it means that in five

---

brood comb, the comb where the eggs are hatched
grub, the form of an insect after it hatches from its egg

days a baby weighing seven and a half pounds to start off with would increase in weight to f i v e   t o n s!'

For the second time, Mrs Taylor stopped knitting.

'But that is only half the story,' Albert said. 'There's more to come. I haven't told you the really *amazing* thing about royal jelly yet. I'm going to show you now how it can *transform* a plain dull-looking little worker bee with practically no *sex organs* at all into a great big beautiful *fertile* queen.'

'Are you saying that our baby is dull-looking and plain?' she asked sharply.

'Now don't go putting words into my mouth, Mabel, please. Just listen to this. Here's how it works. I'll put it very simply for you. The bees want a new queen. So they build an extra large cell, a queen cell, we call it, and they get the old queen to lay one of her eggs in it. The other one thousand nine hundred and ninety-nine eggs she lays in ordinary worker cells. Now, as soon as these eggs hatch into larvae, the nurse bees start feeding them with royal jelly. All of them get it, workers as well as queen. But here's where the difference comes. The worker larvae only receive this special food for the first three days. But not so the larva in the queen cell! It gets royal jelly all through its larval life. The nurse bees simply pour it into the cell, so much in fact that the little larva floats in it. That's what makes it into a queen.'

---

amazing, very surprising
transform, to change completely the appearance or nature of (something or somebody)
sex organs, here, the parts of the queen bee which produce eggs
fertile, producing a lot

'It's pretty hard to believe,' she said, 'that food can do all that.'

'Of course it's hard to believe. It's the greatest *miracle* of the hive. It's such a hell of a big miracle that even the greatest men of science have not been able to explain it.'

He went over to the bookcase and took out a magazine.

'I'm going to find you a few of the reports. Here we are. One of the most famous living doctors of today, Dr Frederick A. Banting became curious about royal jelly. He examined it and found that it contained *dextrose, phenols* . . . well, there's no need to read it all . . . but here it comes – and eighty to eighty-five per cent *unidentified acids*!'

He stood beside the bookcase with the magazine in his hand and a funny little smile on his face. His wife watched him, not knowing what to make of it all.

He was not a tall man; he had a short thick body that was built close to the ground. His head was huge and round, covered with short-cut hair. The greater part of his face – now that he had started growing a beard – was hidden by a *brownish* yellow *fuzz*.

'Eighty to eighty-five per cent,' he said, 'uniden-

---

miracle, wonder; a wonderful happening which has no natural cause or explanation

dextrose, a kind of sugar present in plants and animals

phenol, unidentified acids. There are many kinds of acids, some of which are valuable parts of our food. Phenol is an acid which comes from heavy coal oils, but is also present in royal jelly. The unidentified ones are those we don't know anything about yet.

brownish, rather brown

fuzz, here, soft light hair

tified acids. Isn't that fantastic?'

'What does it mean, unidentified acids?'

'That's the whole point! No one knows! Not even Banting could find out.'

Looking at him now in front of the bookcase, she couldn't help thinking that somehow, in some curious way, there was a touch of bee about this man. She had often seen women grow to look like the horses they rode, and she had noticed that people who had birds or dogs frequently in some small but surprising manner looked like the creature of their choice. But up to now she had never thought that her husband might look like a bee. It shocked her a bit.

'You know something?' she said, staring at him but smiling a little all the same. 'You're getting to look just a little bit like a bee yourself, did you know that?'

He turned and looked at her.

'I suppose it's the beard mostly,' she said. 'I do wish you'd stop wearing it. Even the colour is sort of bee-like, don't you think?'

'What the hell are you talking about, Mabel?'

'Albert,' she said. 'Your language.'

'Do you want to hear any more of this or don't you?'

'Yes, dear, I'm sorry. I was only joking. Do go on.'

He turned away and pulled another magazine out of the bookcase. 'Now just listen to this. "Still and Burdett found that a male rat which had been unable to *breed,* became a father many times over upon receiving a small amount of royal jelly every day."'

'Albert,' she cried, 'this stuff is much too strong to give to a baby! I don't like it at all.'

'Nonsense, Mabel.'

'Then why do they only try it out on rats, tell me that? Why don't some of these famous men of science take it themselves? They're too clever, that's why.'

'But they h a v e given it to people, Mabel. Here's a whole article about it. Listen.' He turned the page and

---

breed, to produce young

began reading from the magazine. "A business man in Mexico City had a very bad case of *psoriasis*. People stopped seeing him. His business began to suffer. He then turned to royal jelly – one drop with every meal – and he was cured within a couple of weeks. A waiter in the Café Jena, also in Mexico City, reported that his father, after taking a small amount of this wonder substance became the father of a boy at the age of ninety . . .'"

'Listen!' Mrs Taylor said, breaking in, 'I think the baby's crying.'

Albert looked up from his reading. Sure enough, the baby was *yelling*.

'She must be hungry,' he said.

His wife looked at the clock. 'Good Lord!' she cried, jumping up. 'It's past her time again already! You mix the feed, Albert, quickly, while I bring her down! But hurry! I don't want to keep her waiting.'

In half a minute, Mrs Taylor was back, carrying the screaming baby in her arms. She was still not used to the noise that a baby makes when it wants its food. 'Do be quick, Albert!' she called, settling herself in the armchair and arranging the child on her lap.

psoriasis, a skin disease
yell, to scream

'Please hurry!'

Albert entered from the kitchen and handed her the bottle of warm milk. 'It's just right,' he said. 'You don't have to test it.'

She pushed the *teat* straight into the wide-open yelling mouth. The baby began to suck. The yelling stopped. Mrs Taylor calmed down.

'Oh, Albert, isn't she lovely?'

'She is, Mabel – thanks to royal jelly.'

'Now dear, I don't want to hear another word about that awful stuff. It frightens me to death.'

'You're making a big mistake,' he said.

'We'll see about that.'

The baby went on sucking the bottle.

'I do believe she's going to finish the whole lot again, Albert.'

'I'm sure she is,' he said.

And a few minutes later, the milk was all gone.

'Oh, what a girl you are!' Mrs Taylor cried, very gently starting to pull out the treat. The baby sensed what she was doing and sucked harder, trying to hold on. The woman gave a quick pull, and p l o p, out it came.

'Waa! Waa! Waa! Waa! Waa!' the baby yelled.

Mrs Taylor put the baby on her shoulded and *patted* its back. It *belched* twice.

'There you are, my darling, you'll be alright now.'

For a few seconds, the yelling stopped. Then it started again.

---

teat, see picture, page 65
pat, to touch gently with the hand
belch, to give out air from the stomach through the mouth

'She's drunk it too quickly,' Albert said.

His wife lifted the baby back to her shoulder. She changed it from side to side. She lay it on its stomach on her lap. She sat it up on her knee. But it didn't belch again, and the yelling became louder and louder every minute.

'There, there, there,' the wife said, kissing the baby.

They waited another five minutes, but not for one moment did the screaming stop.

'Change the *nappy,*' Albert said. 'It's got a wet nappy, that's all.' He fetched a clean one from the kitchen, and Mrs Taylor took the old one off and put the new one on.

'Waa! Waa! Waa! Waa! Waa!' the baby yelled.

'You know what?' Albert said at last.

'What?'

'I believe she's still hungry. How about me fetching her an extra lot?'

'I don't think we ought to do that, Albert.'

'It'll do her good,' he said, getting up from his chair. 'I'm going to warm her up some more.'

He went out into the kitchen and was away several minutes. When he returned he was holding a bottle full of milk.

'I made her a double,' he said. 'Eight ounces. Just in case.'

'Albert! Are you mad! Don't you know it's just as bad to feed her too much as it is to feed her too little?'

'You don't have to give her the lot, Mabel. You can stop any time you like. Go on,' he said, standing over her. 'Give her a drink.'

Mrs Taylor touched the baby's upper lip with the end of the teat. The tiny mouth immediately closed

nappy

teat

over the teat and suddenly there was silence in the
room.

'There you are, Mabel! What did I tell you?'

The woman didn't answer. She was watching the amount of milk in the bottle. It was disappearing fast, and before long three or four ounces out of eight had gone.

'There,' she said. 'That'll do.'

'You can't pull it away now, Mabel.'

'Yes, dear. I must.'

'Go on, woman, give her the rest. She's hungry, can't you see that? Go on, my beauty,' he said. 'You finish the bottle.'

'I don't like it, Albert,' the wife said, but she didn't pull the bottle away.

'She's making up for lost time, Mabel, that's all she's doing.'

Five minutes later the bottle was empty. Slowly, Mrs Taylor took the teat away, and this time there was not a sound from the baby. She lay happily on the mother's lap with her mouth half open.

'Twelve whole ounces, Mabel!' Albert Taylor said. 'Three times the normal amount! Isn't that fantastic!'

The woman was staring down at the baby. And now the old worried look of the frightened mother was slowly returning to her face.

'Come here, Albert,' she said.

He went over and stood beside her.

'Take a good look and tell me if you see anything different.'

He looked closely at the baby. 'She seems bigger, Mabel, if that's what you mean. Bigger and fatter.'

'Hold her,' she ordered. 'Go on, pick her up.'

He lifted the baby up off the mother's lap. 'Good God!' he cried. 'She weighs a ton!'

'Exactly.'

'Now isn't that marvellous!' he cried. 'I'm sure she must be back to normal already!'

'It frightens me, Albert. It's too quick.'

'Nonsense, woman.'

'It's that awful jelly that's done it,' she said. 'I hate the stuff.'

'There's nothing wrong with royal jelly,' he answered.

'Don't be a fool, Albert! Do you think it's normal for a child to start putting on weight at this speed?'

'You're never satisfied!' he cried. 'You're worried sick when she loses weight and now you're frightened to death because she's gaining! What's the matter with you, Mabel?'

The woman got up from her chair with the baby in her arms and started towards the door. 'It's lucky I'm here to see you don't give her any more of it, that's all I can say.' She went out, and Albert watched her through the open door as she crossed the hall to the foot of the stairs. There she suddenly stopped and stood quite still for several seconds as though remembering something. Then she turned and came back rather quickly into the room.

'Albert,' she said. 'There wasn't any royal jelly in this last feed we've just given her, was there?'

'I don't see why there shouldn't be, Mabel.'

'Albert!'

'What's wrong?' he asked softly.

'How d a r e you!' she cried.

Albert Taylor's great bearded face took on a hurt and surprised look. 'I think you ought to be very glad she's got another big bottle of it inside her,' he said.

'Honest I do. And that w a s a big bottle, Mabel, believe you me.'

The woman was standing just inside the doorway holding the sleeping baby in her arms and staring at her husband with huge angry eyes.

'You mark my words,' Albert was saying, 'she'll soon win the first prize in any baby show in the entire country. Hey, why don't you weigh her now and see what she is? You want me to get the scales, Mabel, so you can weigh her?'

The woman walked straight over to the large table in the centre of the room and laid the baby down and quickly started taking off its clothes. 'Yes!' she said angrily. 'Get the scales!'

Then she took off the nappy and threw it away so the baby lay naked on the table.

'But Mabel!' Albert cried. 'It's a miracle! Look how fat she is!'

Indeed, the amount of weight the child had put on since the day before was amazing. Her small *chest* with the *rib bones* showing all over it was now round and fat, and her stomach was *bulging* high in the air. Curiously, though, the child's arms and legs did not seem to have grown the same way. Still short and thin, they looked like little sticks coming out from a ball of fat.

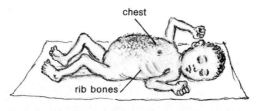

chest

rib bones

---

bulge, to become greater, thicker, like a stomach filled with food

68

'Look!' Albert said. 'She's even beginning to get a bit of fuzz on the stomach to keep her warm!' He put out a hand and was about to run the tips of his fingers over the soft brownish yellow hair that had suddenly appeared on the baby's stomach.

'D o n' t y o u t o u c h h e r!' the woman cried. She turned and faced him with flaming eyes. She looked suddenly like some kind of little fighting bird, ready to fly in his face.

'Now wait a minute,' he said and stepped backwards.

'You must be mad!' she cried.

'Now wait just one minute, Mabel, will you please, because if you're still thinking this stuff is dangerous ... That is what you're thinking, isn't it? All right, then. Listen carefully. I shall now prove to you, once and for all, Mabel, that royal jelly doesn't cause any harm to human beings, even in enormous amounts. For example why do you think we had only half the usual honey crop last summer? Tell me that.'

He was standing three or four yards away from her, where he seemed to feel more comfortable.

'The reason we had only half the usual crop last summer was because I turned one hundred of my hives over to the production of royal jelly.'

'You w h a t?'

'Ah,' he whispered. 'I thought that might surprise you a bit. And I've been making it ever since.' A sly smile was creeping around the corners of his mouth.

'You'll never guess the reason, either,' he said. 'I've been afraid to mention it up to now because I thought it might . . . well . . . sort of embarrass you. You remember that bit I read you out of the magazine?

About the rat that wasn't able to breed ... You get the message, Mabel?' he said with a wide grin.

She stood quite still, facing him.

'The very first time I ever read that sentence, Mabel, I jumped straight out of my chair and I said to myself if it'll work with a rat, I said, then there's no reason on earth why it shouldn't work with Albert Taylor.'

He paused, waiting for his wife to say something. But she didn't.

'And there's another thing,' he went on. 'It made me feel so marvellous, Mabel, so completely different to what I was before that I went right on taking it even after you'd told me you were with child. I've taken lots and lots of it during the last twelve months.'

The big frightened eyes of the woman were moving over the man's face and neck. There was no skin showing at all on his neck. The whole of it, to a point where it disappeared into the shirt, was covered all the way around with soft yellow-black hair.

'Mind you,' he said, looking with love at the baby, 'it's going to work far better on a tiny baby than on a fully developed man like me. You've only got to look at her to see that, don't you agree?'

The woman looked down at the baby. It was lying naked on the table, fat and white and *comatose,* like some enormous grub that would soon end its larval period and come out into the world complete with *mandibles* and wings.

'Why don't you cover her up, Mabel?' he said. 'We don't want our little queen to catch a cold.'

---

comatose, showing hardly any signs of life
mandibles, see picture, page 42

Questions

1. What is unusual about young Albert?

2. How does his interest in bees become a living?

3. What is the problem in his marriage?

4. Why is the mother so worried about her new-born baby?

5. How does Albert think of a way to cure the baby?

6. What is royal jelly?

7. What happens when Albert starts putting it into the baby's milk?

8. How does Mabel feel about it?

9. In what way does royal jelly change the looks of the baby?

10. How does Albert try to prove that royal jelly is not dangerous?

11. Could he be wrong?

Edward the Conqueror

Louisa stepped out of the kitchen door at the back of the house into the cool October sunshine.

bonfire

'Edward!' she called. 'Ed-ward! Lunch is ready!'

She paused a moment and listened; then she walked across the garden. She passed along the flower bed and went all the way along the path until she came to the place where she could look down into the *dip* at the end of this large garden.

brambles

---

dip, here, a small hillside

'Edward! Lunch!'

She could see him now, about eighty yards away, down the dip on the edge of the wood, a tall narrow figure working beside a big *bonfire*. He was throwing *brambles* on to the top of the fire. It was burning fast with orange flames, and the smoke was driven by the wind back over the garden with a wonderful smell of autumn.

Louisa went down towards her husband. If she had wanted, she could easily have called him again and made herself heard. But there was something about a first-class bonfire that drove her towards it, right up close so she could feel the heat and listen to it burn.

'Lunch,' she said as she came nearer.

'Oh, hello. All right – yes. I'm coming.'

'What a good fire.'

'I've decided to clear this place right out,' her husband said. 'I'm sick and tired of all these brambles.'

'You better be careful you don't work too hard, Edward.'

'Louisa, I do wish you would stop treating me as though I were eighty. A bit of exercise never did anyone any harm.'

'Yes, dear, I know. Oh, Edward! Look! Look!'

The man turned and looked at Louisa, who was pointing now to the far side of the bonfire.

'Look, Edward! The cat!'

Sitting on the ground, so close to the fire that the flames seemed to be touching it, was a large cat of a most unusual colour. It stayed quite still, with its head

---

bonfire, brambles, see picture, page 72/73

on one side and its nose in the air, watching the man and the woman with calm yellow eyes.

'It will get burnt!' Louisa cried and ran quickly to it, seized it with both hands, and put it on the grass well clear of the flames.

'You crazy cat,' she said, dusting off her hands. 'What's the matter with you?'

'Cats know what they are doing,' her husband said. 'You will never find a cat doing something it doesn't want. Not cats.'

'Whose is it? Have you ever seen it before?'

'No, I never have. Very unusual colour.'

The cat had seated itself on the grass and was regarding them with a sideways look. It had an air of *contempt,* as though the sight of these two middle-aged persons were a matter of some surprise but very little importance. For a cat, it certainly had an unusual colour – a pure silver-grey with no blue in it at all – and the hair was long and soft.

Louisa bent down and *stroked* its head. 'You must go home,' she said. 'Be a good cat now and go home to where you belong.'

The man and the wife started to walk back up the hill towards the house. The cat got up and followed, at a distance first, but coming closer and closer as they went along. Soon it was alongside them, then it was ahead leading the way across the lawn to the house. It was walking as if it owned the whole place, holding its tail straight up in the air.

'Go home,' the man said. 'We don't want you.'

---

contempt, lack of respect
stroke, to rub gently with the hand

75

But when they reached the house, it came in with them and Louisa gave it some milk in the kitchen. During lunch it jumped up onto the empty chair between them. It sat through the meal with its head just above the table, watching them, its yellow eyes moving slowly from the woman to the man and back again.

'I don't like this cat,' Edward said.

'Oh, I think it's a beautiful cat. I do hope it stays a little while.'

'Now, listen to me, Louisa. The creature can't possibly stay here. It belongs to someone else. It's lost. And if it's still trying to hang around this afternoon, you had better take it to the police. They'll see it gets home.'

After lunch, Edward returned to his garden work. Louisa, as usual, went to the *piano*. She was a good *pianist* and a music lover, and almost every afternoon she spent an hour or so playing for herself. The cat was now lying on the sofa, and she paused to stroke it as she went by. It opened its eyes, looked at her a moment, then closed them again and went back to sleep.

'You're an awfully nice cat,' she said. 'And such a beautiful colour. I wish I could keep you.' Then her fingers, moving over the *fur* on the cat's head, touched a small *lump,* just above the right eye.

'Poor cat,' she said. 'You've got lumps on your beautiful face. You must be getting old.'

---

pianist, one who plays the piano
fur, the skin of certain animals covered with fine hair
lump, here a small round mass on the skin

She went over and sat down on the long *piano stool* but she didn't immediately start to play. One of her special little pleasures was to make a carefully arranged programme every day which she worked out in detail before she began. All she wanted was a short pause after each piece while the audience clapped and called for more. It was so much nicer to imagine an audience. Now and again while she was playing – on her lucky days, that is – the room would become dark and begin to swim. She would see nothing but row upon row of seats and a sea of white faces turned up towards her, listening to her playing.

What should the programme be today? She sat

piano

piano stool

whiskers

cheek

before the piano, a *plump* little person with a round and still quite pretty little face. By looking a little to the right, she could see the cat asleep on the sofa. How about some Bach to begin with? Or, better still, Vivaldi. And perhaps a little Schumann. "Carnaval"*? That would be fun. And after that – well, some Liszt for a change. One of the "Petrarch Sonnets"*. And finally another Schumann – "Kinderszenen"*.

Vivaldi, Schumann, Liszt, Schumann. A very nice programme. Already she could feel that this was one of her lucky days. She moved a little closer to the piano and paused a moment until the audience was quiet. Then she lifted her hands and began to play.

She wasn't watching the cat at all. As a matter of fact she had forgotten its presence, but as the first deep notes of the Vivaldi sounded softly in the room, she noticed, out of the corner of one eye, a sudden movement on the sofa. She stopped playing at once. 'What is it?' she said, turning to the cat. 'What's the matter?'

The animal was no longer asleep. It was sitting upright on the sofa, *quivering*, ears up and eyes wide open, staring at the piano.

'Did I frighten you?' she asked gently. 'Perhaps you've never heard music before?'

No, she told herself. I don't think that's what it is. The cat didn't seem afraid. It didn't back away. If anything it leaned forward. And the face – well, there was a rather strange expression on the face of surprise

---

plump, a little fat
* titles of pieces of music
quiver, to shake

or shock. Of course the face of a cat is a small thing that doesn't show much expression. But if you watch carefully the eyes and the ears working together, you can sometimes see signs of very strong *emotions*. Louisa was watching the face closely now, and because she was curious to see what would happen a second time, she reached out her hands and began again to play the Vivaldi.

This time the cat was ready for it, and to begin with it just sat up very straight. But as the music went on a strange look almost of *ecstasy* settled upon the cat's face. The head went over to one side, and its eyes were half closed. At that moment Louisa was certain that the animal was really *appreciating* the work.

What she saw – or thought she saw – was something she had noticed many times on the faces of people who listen closely to a piece of music. When the sound takes complete hold of them, and drowns them in itself, a strange look of ecstasy comes over them. You can recognize it as easily as a smile. So far as Louisa could see, the cat was now wearing almost exactly this kind of look.

When the piece was over and the music stopped, there could be no doubt anymore that the cat had been listening. It moved about a little and stretched a leg. Then it settled into a more comfortable position and looked in her direction as if expecting something. It was just what a human being would do in the pause between two pieces of music.

---

emotion, any feeling of love, hate, fear, or the like
ecstasy, very great pleasure
appreciate, to understand the worth of (something)

'You like that?' she asked. 'You like Vivaldi?'

The moment she had spoken, she felt *ridiculous,* but not – and this was a little frightening – not quite so ridiculous as she knew she should have felt.

Well, there was nothing for it now except to go straight ahead with the next number on the programme, which was "Carnaval". As soon as she began to play, the cat sat up straight. Then as the sound slowly took hold of it, it fell back again into a strange mood of ecstasy. It was really a fantastic sight – quite a funny one, too – to see this silver-grey cat sitting on the sofa and being carried away like this. And what made it more crazy than ever, Louisa thought, was that this music, which the animal seemed to be enjoying so much, was too difficult, too *classical* to be appreciated by most humans in the world.

The cat seemed to be following every single note. It was certainly a fantastic thing. But was it not also a wonderful thing? Indeed it was. In fact, unless she was much mistaken, it was a kind of miracle. It was one of those animal miracles that happen about once every hundred years.

'I could see you loved that one,' she said when the piece was over. 'I'm sorry I didn't play it too well today. Which did you like best, the Vivaldi or the Schumann?'

The cat made no reply. Louisa, fearing she might lose its attention went straight into the next part of the programme – Liszt's second "Petrarch sonnet".

---

ridiculous, very silly; to be laughed at
classical, (of music) serious

Now a strange thing happened. She hadn't played more than a few seconds when the animal's *whiskers* began to *twitch*. Slowly it drew itself up to an extra height. It laid its head on one side, then on the other, and stared into space with a look of wonder that seemed to say, 'What is this? Don't tell me. I know it so well, but just for the moment I don't seem to be able to place it ...' Louisa was *fascinated,* and with her little mouth half open and half smiling, she continued to play, waiting to see what on earth was going to happen next.

The cat stood up, walked to one end of the sofa, sat down again, listened some more. Then at once it jumped to the floor and up onto the piano stool beside her. There it sat, listening with attention to the lovely music, its large yellow eyes fixed upon Louisa's fingers.

'Well!' she said when she had finished. 'So you came up to sit beside me, did you? You like this better than the sofa? All right, I'll let you stay, but you must keep still and not jump about.'

She put one hand out and stroked the cat softly along the back, from head to tail. 'That was Liszt,' she said. Then she went on to the next piece on the programme, Schumann's "Kinderszenen".

She hadn't been playing for more than a minute or two when she realized that the cat had again moved, and was now back in its old place on the sofa. She had

---

whiskers, see picture, page 77
twitch, to make a sudden small movement
fascinate, to interest very strongly

been watching her hands at the time, and that was probably why she hadn't noticed its going. The cat was still staring at her and listening closely to the music. Yet it seemed to Louisa that it didn't show the same interest in this piece as in the Liszt.

'What's the matter?' she asked when it was over. 'What's so marvellous about Liszt?' The cat looked straight back at her with those yellow eyes with small black bars in their centres.

This, she told herself, is really beginning to get interesting, and frightening, too.

'All right,' she said. 'I'll tell you what I'm going to do. I'm going to change my programme specially for you. You seem to like Liszt so much, I'll give you another.'

Softly she began to play one more piece by Liszt. She was now watching the cat very closely. The first thing she noticed was that the whiskers again began to twitch. It jumped down to the floor and stood still for a moment, quivering in ecstasy. Then it walked around the piano, jumped up on the stool, and sat down beside her.

They were in the middle of all this when Edward came in from the garden.

'Edward!' Louisa cried, jumping up. 'Oh, Edward, darling! Listen to this! Listen to what has happened!'

'What is it now?' he said. 'I'd like some tea.' His long narrow face was shining with sweat.

'It's the cat!' Louisa cried, pointing to it sitting quietly on the piano stool. 'Just wait till you hear what has happened!'

'I thought I told you to take it to the police.'

'But, Edward, listen to me. It's terribly exciting.

This is a *musical* cat.'

'Oh, yes?'

'This cat can appreciate music, and it can understand it too.'

'Now stop this nonsense, Louisa, and for God's sake let's have some tea. I'm hot and tired from cutting brambles and building bonfires.' He sat down in an armchair, took a cigarette from a box beside him, and lit it.

'What you don't understand,' Louisa said, 'is that something extremely exciting has been happening here in our own house while you were out. It is something that may even be . . . well . . . of great importance.'

'I'm quite sure of that.'

'Edward, please!'

Louisa was standing by the piano, quite red in her little face. 'If you want to know,' she said, 'I'll tell you what I think.'

'I'm listening, dear.'

'I think it might be possible that we are at this moment sitting in the presence of . . .' She stopped, as though she suddenly sensed how *absurd* the thought was.

'Yes?'

'You may think it silly, Edward, but it's honestly what I think.'

'In the presence of whom, for heaven's sake?'

'Of Franz Liszt himself!'

---

musical, here, who appreciates music
absurd, silly; clearly wrong

Her husband took a long slow pull at his cigarette and blew the smoke out in the room. Every time he took a pull at the cigarette his *cheeks* went in and the bones of his face stood out like a *skeleton's*. 'I don't get you,' he said.

'Edward, listen to me. From what I've seen this afternoon with my own eyes, it really seems to be some sort of *reincarnation.'*

'You mean this silly cat?'

'Don't talk like this, dear, please.'

'You are not ill, are you, Louisa?'

'I'm perfectly all right, thank you very much. I'm a bit *confused* – I don't mind admitting it, but who wouldn't be after what's just happened?'

'What did happen, if I may ask?'

Louisa told him, and while she was talking her husband leaned back in the chair with his legs stretched out in front of him. He was smoking his cigarette and blowing the smoke out in the room. There was a thin *cynical* smile on his mouth.

'I don't see anything very unusual about that,' he said when it was over. 'All it is – is a trick cat. It's been taught tricks, that's all.'

'Don't be so silly, Edward. Every time I play Liszt, he gets all excited and comes running over to sit on

---

cheek, see picture, page 77
skeleton, together the bones form the skeleton
reincarnation means that the soul of the dead comes back in another body
confused, you are confused if a problem or a situation is too diffi-cult to understand
cynical, having a low opinion of human nature

the stool beside me. But only for Liszt, and nobody can teach a cat the difference between Liszt and Schumann. You don't even know it yourself. But this one can do it every single time.'

'Twice,' her husband said. 'He's only done it twice.'

'Twice is enough.'

'Let us see him do it again. Come on.'

'No,' Louisa said. 'Certainly not. Because if this is Liszt, or the soul of Liszt or whatever it is that comes back, then it is not right to put him through a lot of silly tests.'

'My dear woman! This is a cat – a rather *stupid* grey cat that nearly got its coat burned by the bonfire this morning in the garden. And, anyway, what do you know about reincarnation?'

'If his soul is there, that's enough for me,' Louisa said firmly. 'That's all that counts.'

'Come on. Let's see him perform. Let's see him tell the difference between his own stuff and someone else's.'

'No, Edward. I've told you before, I refuse to put him through any more silly circus tests. He has had quite enough of that for one day. But I'll tell you what I'll do. I'll play him a little more of his own music.'

'That won't prove anything.'

'You watch. And one thing is certain – as soon as he recognizes it, he'll refuse to get off that stool where he is sitting now.'

Louisa went to the music shelf, took down a book of Liszt, went through it quickly, and chose a piece. She had meant to play only some of it. But once she got

---

stupid, foolish, not clever

started and saw how the cat was sitting there quivering with pleasure and watching her hands with attention, she didn't have the heart to stop. She played it all the way through. When it was finished, she looked up at her husband and smiled. 'There you are,' she said. 'You can't tell me he wasn't absolutely loving it.'

'He just likes the noise, that's all.'

'He was loving it. Weren't you, darling?' she said and lifted the cat in her arms. 'Oh, dear, if only he could talk. Just think of it, dear, he met Beethoven when he was young! He knew Schumann and Mendelssohn and Grieg and Heine and Balzac. And let me see . . . My heavens, he was Wagner's *father-in-law!* I'm holding Wagner's father-in-law in my arms!'

'Louisa!' her husband said in a sharp voice, sitting up straight. 'Pull yourself together.' There was a new note in his voice now, and he spoke louder.

Louisa looked up quickly. 'Edward, I do believe you're *jealous!*'

'Of a stupid grey cat!'

'Then stop being so *grumpy* and cynical about it all. And if you won't, then the best thing you can do is to go back to your own garden work and leave the two of us together in peace. That will be the best for all of us, won't it, darling?' she said and stroked the cat on its head. 'And later on this evening,' she said to the cat,

---

father-in-law, the father of one's husband or wife. (Liszt's daughter was married to Wagner)

jealous, here, afraid of losing his wife's love and attention to the cat

grumpy, angry

'we shall have some more music together, you and I, some more of your own work. Oh, yes,' she said and kissed the cat on the neck, 'and we might have a little Chopin, too. You needn't tell me, I know you love Chopin. You used to be great friends with him, didn't you, darling? So you shall have some Chopin,' she said and kissed the cat again.

'Louisa, stop this at once!'

'Oh, don't be so stuffy, Edward.'

'You're making a complete fool of yourself, woman. And anyway, you forget we're going out this evening, to Bill and Betty's to play cards.'

'Oh, but I couldn't possibly go out now. There's no question of that.'

Edward got up slowly from his chair. 'Tell me something,' he said quietly. 'You don't really believe this – this nonsense you're talking, do you?'

'But of course I do. I don't think there's any question about it now.'

'You know what I think,' he said, 'I think you ought to see a doctor. And quick, too.'

With that he turned and walked out of the room, through the garden door.

Louisa watched him walking across the lawn towards his bonfire and his brambles. She waited until he was out of sight before she turned and ran to the front door with the cat in her arms.

Soon she was in the car, driving to town.

She parked in front of the library, and locked the cat in the car. Then she hurried up the steps into the building. She began searching the cards for two subjects – REINCARNATION and LISZT. Under REINCARNATION she found something called

"Recurring Earth-Lives – how and why", by a man called F. Milton Willis, from 1921. Under LISZT she found two *biographies.* She took out all three books, returned to the car, and drove home.

Back in the house, she placed the cat on the sofa, sat herself down beside it with her three books, and prepared to do some serious reading. She decided she would begin with Mr F. Milton Willis's work.

The soul, she read, passes from higher to higher

---

recurring, that happens again and again
biography, a written account of the life of a person

forms of animals. "A man cannot be *reborn* as an animal."

She read this again. But how did he know? How could he be so sure? He couldn't. No one could possibly be certain about a thing like that. At the same time, the statement took a great deal of the wind out of her sails.

She read some more that she didn't understand at all, but she read on. Soon she came to an interesting passage that told how long a soul usually stayed away from the earth before returning in someone else's body. According to Mr Willis this depended on a person's social position and "the highest class of gentlemen farmers" were just about the most *superior* beings on earth. The time before they returned was 600 to 1000 years.

Quickly she took one of the other books to find out how long Liszt had been dead. It said he died in Bayreuth in 1886. That was sixty-seven years ago. Therefore, according to Mr Willis, he would have to have been an "unskilled worker" to come back so soon. That didn't seem to fit at all. No, she thought, that isn't right. It was a pleasure to find herself doubting Mr Willis.

Later on in the book, she came upon a list of some of the more famous reincarnations. Cicero, she was told, returned to earth as Gladstone, Alfred the Great came back as Queen Victoria, William the Conqueror as Lord Kitchener. "Theodore Roosevelt," it said, "has for numbers of incarnations played great parts as

---

reborn, born again
superior, of a higher quality

leaders of men . . . Roosevelt and Caesar have been together time after time; many thousands of years ago, they were husband and wife . . ."

That was enough for Louisa. Mr F. Milton Willis was clearly guessing. The fellow was probably right about certain things but some of his statements were simply wrong, in particular the first one of all, about animals. Now she could prove that a man could indeed come back as a lower animal. Also that he did not have to be an unskilled worker to come back within a hundred years.

She now turned to one of the Liszt biographies. She was looking through it when her husband came in again from the garden.

'What are you doing now?' he asked.

'Oh, just checking up a little here and there. Listen, my dear, did you know that Theodore Roosevelt once was Caesar's wife?'

'Louisa,' he said, 'look – why don't you stop this nonsense? I don't like to see you making a fool of yourself like this. Give me that stupid cat and I'll take it to the police station myself.'

Louisa didn't seem to hear him. She was staring at a picture of Liszt in the book. 'My God!' she cried. 'Edward, look!'

'What?'

'Look! The *warts* on his face! I forgot all about them! He had these great warts on his face and it was a famous thing.'

'Oh, Christ!' the man said.

---

wart, a small hard lump on the skin

'The cat has them, too! Look, I'll show you.'

She took the animal in her arms. 'There! There's one! And there's another! Wait a minute! I do believe they are in the same places! Where's that picture?'

It was a famous painting of the *musician* in his old

age with long grey hair that covered his ears and came halfway down his neck. On the face itself, each large wart was shown, and there were five of them in all.

'Now, in the picture there's one above the right eye.' She looked at the cat. 'Yes! It's here! Even in the same place. And another one on the left, at the top of the nose. That one is there, too! And one just below it on the cheek. And two close together on the right side. Edward! Look! They are exactly the same.'

'It doesn't prove a thing.'

She looked up at her husband who was standing in the centre of the room, still wet with sweat. 'You're *scared,* aren't you, Edward? Scared of losing your precious *dignity* and having people think you are making a fool of yourself just for once.'

'I refuse to get *hysterical* about it, that's all.'

'Edward, this is the most wonderful thing that has

---

musician, one who plays music
scared, afraid
dignity, manner showing a sense of one's own worth
hysterical, so upset that you lose control over yourself

ever happened!' she cried, holding the cat in her arms. 'Isn't it marvellous to think we've got Franz Liszt staying in the house?'

'Now, Louisa. Don't let's get hysterical.'

'I can't help it. I simply can't. And to imagine that he's going to live with us for always.'

'I beg your pardon?'

'Oh, Edward! Isn't it exciting. And do you know what I'm going to do next? Every musician in the whole world is going to want to meet him, that's a fact, and ask him about the people he knew – about Beethoven and Chopin and Schubert . . .'

'He can't talk,' her husband said.

'Well, all right. But they're going to want to meet him anyway, just to see him and touch him and to play their own music to him, modern music he's never heard before. They'll come flying from every corner of the earth!'

'To see a grey cat?'

'Darling, it's the same thing. It's h i m. No one cares what he looks like. Oh, Edward, it'll be the most exciting thing there ever was!'

'They'll think you're mad.'

'You wait and see.' She was holding the cat in her arms and stroking it. Her husband walked over to the garden door and stood there staring out in the garden. The evening was beginning. The lawn was turning slowly from green to black, and in the distance he could see the smoke from his bonfire.

'No,' he said, without turning around, 'I'm not having it. Not in this house. It'll make us both look perfect fools.'

'Edward, what do you mean?'

'Just what I say. I absolutely refuse to let you tell anybody about this foolish thing. You happen to have found a trick cat. O.K. That's fine. Keep it, if it pleases you. I don't mind. But let that be as far as it goes. Do you understand me, Louisa? I don't want to hear any more of this crazy talk.'

Louisa put the cat slowly down on the sofa. Then slowly she raised herself to her full small height and took one step forward. 'Damn you, Edward!' she shouted. 'For the first time in our lives something really exciting comes along and you're scared to death of having anything to do with it because somebody may laugh at you! That's right, isn't it?'

'Louisa,' her husband said. 'That's quite enough of that. Pull yourself together now and stop this at once. We've had too many of these scenes. I know that this may be a difficult time of life for you, and that . . .'

'Oh, my God! You idiot! You pompous idiot! Can't you see that this is different, this is – something of a miracle? Can't you see that?' She had tears in her eyes.

At that point, he came across the room and took her by the shoulders. He had a cigarette between his lips, and she could see the marks on his skin where the sweat had dried. 'Listen,' he said. 'I'm hungry. I've been working all day in the garden, and I'm tired and hungry and I want some supper. So do you. Off you go now to the kitchen and get us something good to eat.'

Louisa stepped back and put both hands to her mouth. 'My heavens!' she cried. 'I forgot all about it. He must be absolutely starved. Except for some milk, I haven't given him a thing to eat since he arrived.'

'Who?'

'Why, h i m, of course. I must go at once and cook

something really special. What do you think he would like best, Edward?'

'D a m n y o u, Louisa!'

'Now, Edward, please. I'm going to handle this m y way just for once. You stay here,' she said, bending down and touching the cat gently with her fingers. 'I won't be long.'

Louisa went into the kitchen and stood wondering what special *dish* she should prepare. How about a *soufflé*? Yes, that would be rather special. Of course, Edward didn't care much for them, but that couldn't be helped.

She was only a fair cook, and she couldn't be sure of always having a soufflé come out well. But she took extra trouble this time. When it was ready she carried it into the living-room. As she entered, she saw her husband coming in through the garden door.

'Here's his supper,' she said, putting it on the table and turning towards the sofa. 'Where is he?'

Her husband closed the garden door behind him and walked across the room to get himself a cigarette.

'Edward, where is he?'

'Who?'

'You know who.'

'Ah, yes. Yes, that's right. Well – I'll tell you.' He was lighting his cigarette. He looked up and saw Louisa looking at him – at his shoes and at the bottom of his trousers, which were wet from walking in the grass.

'I just went out to see how the bonfire was going,' he said.

---

dish, a particular kind of food
soufflé, a kind of light cooked dish made with beaten egg whites

Her eyes travelled slowly up and rested on his hands.

'It's still burning fine,' he went on. 'I think it'll keep going all night.'

But the way she was staring made him uncomfortable.

'What is it?' he said and put the lighter down. Then he looked down and noticed for the first time the long thin *scratch* that ran across the back of one hand.

'Edward!'

'Yes,' he said. 'I know. Those brambles are terrible. They tear you to pieces. Now, just a minute, Louisa. What's the matter?'

'Edward!'

'Oh, for God's sake, woman! Sit down and keep calm. There's nothing to get worked up about. Louisa! Louisa, s i t   d o w n!'

---

scratch, a thin wound on the surface of the skin

Questions

1. What is Edward doing in the garden?
2. What does he want to do with the cat Louisa finds?
3. How does Louisa spend her afternoons?
4. In what way is this a "lucky day" for Louisa?
5. How does the cat show its interest in music?
6. Which music does it prefer?
7. What does that lead Louisa to believe?
8. How does Edward explain the way the cat is acting?
9. What does Louisa hope to find in the books from the library?
10. What does she plan to do?
11. Why don't Louisa's plans suit her husband?
12. What does the cat mean to Louisa?
13. What does the cat mean to Edward?
14. How do you see the ending?